# IT:
## THE UGLY ICKY STUFF

*And How I Learned to Trust*

**ELIZABETH GRANT**

WESTBOW
PRESS®
A DIVISION OF THOMAS NELSON
& ZONDERVAN

This is a creative nonfiction work. The events are described to the best of Elizabeth Grant's memory. Although the stories are true, the names have been changed to protect the privacy of the people involved.

WestBow Press books may be ordered through booksellers or by contacting:

WestBow Press
A Division of Thomas Nelson & Zondervan
1663 Liberty Drive
Bloomington, IN 47403
www.westbowpress.com
1 (866) 928-1240

Scripture quotations are from the ESV® Bible (The Holy Bible, English Standard Version®), copyright © 2001 by Crossway, a publishing ministry of Good News Publishers. Used by permission. All rights reserved.

ISBN: 978-1-9736-8078-9 (sc)
ISBN: 978-1-9736-8079-6 (e)

Library of Congress Control Number: 2019919744

Print information available on the last page.

WestBow Press rev. date: 12/12/2019

# INTRODUCTION

*T*his is a little book on the author's past experiences. This memoir is to inspire and explain how certain life struggles can be difficult. The author portrays the growth, hope, and trust that is found through life's ups and downs.

# FOREWORD

*I*n this personal work, Elizabeth McCormack Grant shares her journey to sobriety, spirituality, and love. Bravely, she shares her innermost vulnerabilities through her growth as a human being seeking acceptance and forgiveness from others and herself. Her story is simply told, but it is a piece that will resonate with her readers whether they share her experiences or not.

By; Wendy Cipriotti

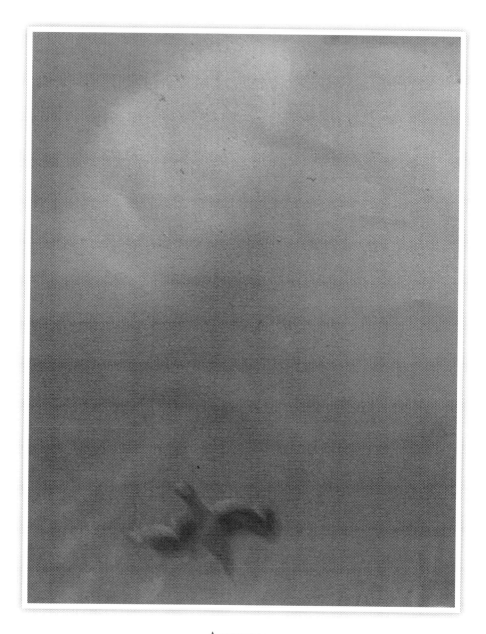

Awareness

# ACKNOWLEDGEMENTS

O n the completion of this work, I would like to give thanks to God who has guided me to work on myself. This book would not have been possible without the love and support from my family and friends who encouraged me. This has been a wonderful process for me, and for that I am truly grateful.

*W*e all have been heartbroken in relationships. As humans, we long for a connection that is hard to describe. Our journey in search of the existence of love starts. We know it must be true by the books we read, the stories we learn, and plays like Romeo and Juliet that we absorb. Although Romeo and Juliet is a tragedy, the storyline conveys love-peace between the two houses. Do I have your attention? Yes you, the one reading.

"Trust in the Lord with all your heart" (English Standard Bible, Prov. 3.5). I learned this lesson at forty-seven years old. I trusted God with almost everything, but not the It- the ugly, icky stuff buried inside the depth of the dark place, an imperfect self. It was mine. The pain is what I call it. It was similar to Golam's ring, "My precious! It's mine!" I am here to share my hope and experience in how I learned to love and trust through my journey in overcoming life's challenges.

Why are humans creatures of habit? We live in a world where

fear, doubt, hate, dysfunction, misunderstanding, and judgment are taught to us from the moment we reach an age in which the opinions of others matter. We all desire happiness in our lives, yet all too often we look for people and things of this world to fill this place in our hearts. Why do we allow the circumstances of outside forces to crypt us as individuals? It- the ugly, icky stuff no one likes to admit or talk about. It caused me to remain in chains of insecurity, a feeling so aggravating and embarrassing that it disabled me into being lazy and so full of resentment that I would not finish the things I started. College was never completed due to a lack of confidence in myself to pass even math. It- the ugly, icky stuff consumed me. It was my way of thinking that influenced my reactions and actions. It was the self-condemning negative talk I told myself, that kept me in a never ending pattern of bondage, self-destruction, and despair.

As a girl, I behaved like someone who knew it all but was naïve to suggestions. I misunderstood kindness and confused caring for love. When I was young, I was diagnosed with epilepsy that affected the way I interacted with others. I was shy with no confidence and possessed an inability to trust others or communicate my feelings. I was sad being pulled out of five different elementary schools before going to a school for my special needs, and consequently, defeated with the disappointment of not being able to go to school with my own twin sister until junior high school. Then my older sister got married and I would only see her during the holidays. Though I was thankful for the time we spent together, I was again saddened by not having her closer. I was the kind of kid who used to sing made up songs to God while playing on the swings, but became a girl no one understood and picked on. I carried scars like millions of girls do, and yes, they were hidden. I did not talk about them because it just hurt too much to do so. The thought of addressing these demons would cross my mind but left just as quickly as the thought came. We all know that childhood is not a picnic, and many of us just wish there was a genie in a lamp nearby to grant our wish to be a different age than the one we were trapped in. During my childhood and adolescents, I struggled in forming and keeping friendships due to my debilitating lack of trust. It came as no surprise that

After struggling through a difficult and painful childhood of mistrust, life turned from bad to worse shortly after I got married in 1994. However, I had moments of a powerful presence in my life. Early in the year, my husband Alex and I travelled from Michigan, and as we approached the Colorado Rockies, a light came through the clouds. A presence of peace rested upon my heart. I knew I would be back in California and maybe I would put the past behind me. If Alex had any idea of the deceit I had committed, he would hate me. I was not being honest with him about my infidelity, and as a result, I was wallowing in guilt. Once we settled after the move, he tried to make it work between us. He would take me out for dinner, like we were courting again. Notwithstanding, I was completely unwilling to forgive myself. Self-sabotaging was something I did automatically, I just did not realize it. By 1995, I abandoned my marriage and we filed for divorce. Maybe this was to protect him from any further harm I could have caused him. A failed marriage was added to It- the ugly, icky stuff. A collection of resentments, hurts, disappointments, and unfinished business. I was facing a constant battle deep within myself. I lacked a fundamental quality in relationships. Simply, trust. It- the ugly, icky stuff caused me to become angry, cursing and yelling at those who were around me. I thought I was a quitter. I admitted to myself the nature of my wrongs, even though internally I told myself he deserves better. I was even impatient with people that worked in stores due to my own frustrations in the circumstances I was experiencing.

In 1996, I entered another relationship, thinking it would fix all my worries and fill the constant void that was missing in my heart. I fell in love and felt alive again. However, I did not think I deserved to find love so soon after leaving my ex-husband. We shared a lot in common. I am a twin, and so is he. His middle name began with the same initial letter as my middle name. He was the older twin, and I was born before my sister by ten minutes. Similarly, we shared the same feelings of inadequacy in our families. Frank and I did everything together: concerts, amusement parks, family gatherings. We never were apart, as Frank's happiness meant more to me than the thought of my own. The feeling of belonging came natural for us. His unbelievable talent with music and knowledge of mathematics blew me away. I sparkled when I heard his name. Nonetheless, in the eleventh month of our courtship, we decided to take a time out from each other. I was again in pain. My soul felt despair. As I floundered through this relationship, I chose to start suppressing It- the ugly, icky stuff by drinking and using drugs. I then formed a relationship with my addiction. As a result, I lied to the very people who loved me. I watched all of my relationships fall apart as a result of not trusting in the right things.

Then in 1997, during the first year of my drug abuse, Angel, a friend of mine, introduced me to her boyfriend. It triggered things of my childhood I had not healed or moved on from. I still remember my first encounter with her Italian boyfriend, Anthony. My initial reaction was that he looked exactly like Michael Keaton or George Clooney. I quickly noticed he was kind-hearted, intelligent, and unique. He seemed to be reliable as a friend and a humble partner to Angel. He filled his apartment with the books and music he owned. Three pictures hung on his wall which reminded me of my childhood. The scent of Aqua Di Gio (Giorgio Armani) lingered in the living room and hallway near the bathroom. The passion Anthony expressed towards his family and his love for music was conspicuous. The calmness of his voice seemed encouraging, and I learned that we both shared the same perspective on relationships: we stay until we cannot stay anymore. We shared the same story. Additionally, I was currently keeping my drug addiction a secret from Frank, my current boyfriend. I confided in Angel and Anthony about my feelings about my relationship with my boyfriend. It was comforting to be able to share this with them. I recall being shocked and feeling a strong connection to both of them, as we had similar relationship struggles. I spent a lot of time with them, sometimes barbecuing, sometimes including Frank. In 1999, I learned that Angel had moved out of state and as a result she and Anthony ended their relationship. My boyfriend and I, however, were still together.. But in May 2000, once again, I ended another relationship due to my drug addiction. Frank and I were over. My heart was completely shattered, though I knew that I was a contributing factor to why the relationship ended. I found myself couch surfing and in a way homeless. I quickly understood the importance of independence and started working excessively to save up money to get into an apartment. Slowly, the feeling of self-worth gave me hope for the future.

Although in spite of the improvements I was attempting to make on October 31, 2000, I contacted Anthony and apologized for my selfish and inconsiderate behavior because I was using and drinking. "You don't have anything to be sorry for. Can we have coffee sometime?" What he said and how he said it resonated with me. I made it known that I was only using on weekends and gave him my work and my pager numbers. Three days later while I was cleaning my apartment, the phone rang. I answered and was shocked to hear, "Liz I am coming over." Anthony's voice seemed unfamiliar, with a formality as though he was making a public announcement.

When Anthony arrived, our chemistry together was immediate. We exchanged ideas and shared feelings of our past hurts. I started to realize that I did not need to drink or party to hang out with anyone. Although Anthony was drinking water. When we were simply talking to each other I noticed a genuine caring. We both laughed, listened to music, and played cards. The evening was one of the best nights I have ever had. While playing cards, the conversation we shared impacted me. Anthony spoke to me philosophically and his approach to life resonated with me. Although in my heart, I was not emotionally available to react the way I should have. "You are going to feel pain for a reason," he said firmly. These were words that reached the ache inside me, and I felt as though God had spoken through him. Anthony encouraged me to forgive and let things go.

*Elizabeth Grant*

The reality of the situation was that I was still sick and unwilling to face myself. I wanted to know what he really thought of me, but that alone frightened me. Somehow, something brilliant was happening as a result of the incredible words he said to me. Meanwhile, at this same time, my twin sister was about to give birth. There was a connection with my thoughts and my sister's new baby- a rebirth of my very spirit.

The day before my twin sister went into labor, the thought replayed in my mind: I was going to feel pain. I fell to my knees in the middle of my living room as a tape was played for me to view in my mind. It was a rude awakening in which I felt unworthy to experience. Would anyone even believe me? I confided in my dad by telling him what happened with Anthony. My dad said to me, "Miff, he sure seems like a good friend to have." I began to cry, because I knew my father was right. My dad added, "Liz if you cry over someone it means you care. Tell Anthony you care."

This awakening led me to join the Catholic Church. Through a connection with Anthony, I found a sponsor to join the congregation and as a result worked on getting sober. Attending a weekly group in RCIA (Rite of Christian Initiation of Adults) ministry was something that was encouraging me to be a better person.

In spite of the improvements I was making, I received a page from a number in January 2001 that I did not recognize, but called my voicemail anyway. It seemed logical to leave a message and find out who it was. Not long after, my pager went off again. This communication exchange was intriguing, but I still had no idea who it was. Shortly after, my landline rang and it was a guy clearly attempting to disguise his voice. For months and months the paging and early morning prank calls continued, but I chose not to engage. I felt helpless and emotionally played. I was confused, hurt, and taunted by the way it impacted me. It- the ugly, icky stuff caused me to lash out and blame people as I was trying to identify an enemy without having proof. For this reason, I felt depressed. I started using again, and went to RCIA less and less. My drug addiction wrecked my relationships with family and friends all over again.

It- the ugly, icky stuff showed up in the way I made decisions that left me in situations I would not normally be in. Later that year, I was evicted from my apartment and found out I was pregnant. The physical abuse with drugs caused me to bleed for several months. Doctors told me that I would not have the baby I was carrying, and just as devastating, this baby was conceived with someone I did not love. In November 2001, I miscarried on my father's birthday. I just wanted to live my life again as a Catholic. Instead, I overreacted when I was not getting the attention I wanted from Anthony and I became angry.

It was later in May the following year that I reconnected with my

Anthony's friend's mother from church. I was back in California and I felt it was time for me to finish what I started. It was humbling and humiliating, all at the same time. I felt I was judged and not accepted. Additionally, none of my acquaintances or friends had any idea of Anthony's whereabouts. Nevertheless, in 2003, I was confirmed into the Catholic faith and was elated over my success. At confirmation, I shared that the next goal was a twelve step program, which heartened my sponsor, as she knew I struggled with addiction.

Yet later in that year, I was desperate and needed help with my addiction. I attended meetings and was frustrated because I still ended up using. In my helplessness, I attempted to reconnect with Anthony through his friends; I was repeatedly told that the family did not know where to find him. I, however, did find him. He was in Northern California. I let everyone in his life know that I was going, and they should let him know.

For the second time, Anthony encouraged me, saying, "If you want to be my friend Liz, you need to quit." I heard him this time and so I started on a journey to wholeness. I committed to my program, got involved in the activities, read and wrote as I went through the twelve steps. The powerful presence in my life was still there. On my forty-fifth day clean and sober, and on my mother and father's forty-fifth wedding anniversary, my father died of a massive heart attack. If I was going to relapse, it would have been during this painful process. My dad believed in me, just like Anthony. The pain of losing my father was suffocating. At this same time, the fires in Ventura County were blazing so my twin sister and her husband picked me up to travel to Prescott Valley, Arizona. I felt choked when I remembered the last time I talked to my dad and the last time I was in Arizona. It- the ugly, icky stuff was front and center, reminding me of the moments I let my dad down. As we made our journey, I thought of everything I wanted to say and the things I should not have said to my dad. The tape of negative feelings played as I got closer to Prescott Valley.

In that pain, I yearned for comfort from Anthony. Yet, a miracle of healing took place out of this painful experience. I was taken to my first meeting on McCormick Road in Arizona by a relative who made an apology to me. Later, I was asked by my family to stay on for three to four weeks with my mom and relatives visiting from England. It- ugly, icky stuff placed doubts in my mind of my ability to help anyone. Regardless, I agreed and stayed as long as my mom needed me. "Yeah, ask the drug addict sister to take care of mom," I sarcastically laughed. I drove my family to the Grand Canyon to find a view that was breathtaking. The last time I was there was with my dad and mom. In both experiences, I witnessed God's beauty. This time, while marveling at the Grand Canyon, I was within feet of a herd of deer. I got to be fully present and available to enjoy the moment. A few weeks later, my mom and I drove home to California for the holidays, during which a healing took place between us. I was very new to the recovery process, and still had a lot of work ahead of me, but was grateful for the small miracle that happened during my time in Arizona.

In the summer of 2004, It- the ugly, icky stuff presented itself again in my behavior. In recovery, I learned that I carried certain types of character defects. To name a few: impatience, unwillingness, distrust, fear, and pride. I was in contact with Anthony during the first year of my recovery. I called him to ask for advice and learned that he moved to out of state. This was strange, disappointing, and heartbreaking because he was so encouraging and upfront with me. I was left with blame and guilt, feeling unloved and worthless because he did not bother to say goodbye. It- the ugly, icky stuff caused me to carry feelings of anger, fear, rejection, and abandonment. In that moment I buried the pain. The pain would now be like a haunting for the next fourteen years. It- the ugly, icky stuff caused me to be obsessed with my thoughts of him and I could not and would not forgive myself. Why did he vanish? How could he do this? Doesn't he understand how much he means to me? These were words I could never tell him.

For the next two years, I worked hard on my life. It- the ugly, icky stuff was always there. I still carried the hurt from Anthony. I worked through my other hurts by attending my twelve steps program, staying involved more with the Catholic Church, and taking on commitments in program. I spite of moments of peace, deep down I was still burying the hurt.

In 2005, I moved into a rental and contacted my sponsor from church because it was Thanksgiving. Her grandson had died suddenly and I was asked to attend the funeral. At that moment, I knew that I would have an opportunity to see Anthony. It- the ugly, icky stuff was still there and I began to feel things I did not want to feel. All I needed to do was show up and be in the moment for my sponsor, not be distracted with the mystery of him vanishing from my life. At the funeral I simply showed up and paid my respect to the grieving family, while not reacting to what was being displayed by him as an act. It- the ugly, icky stuff caused me to be in more pain than I was to begin with. It was as though someone ripped off the Band-Aid from a wound that was trying to heal. I left with a pit in my stomach, and as I drove away I began to cry.

I felt it was time for a change that following year in 2006. I started to heal from the prior year. I was in the process of making amends to various people in my life and reached out to my ex-boyfriend, Frank. After a brief rekindling of our friendship, we discovered that a romantic relationship was not a part of the plan. What a blessing. I had been clean and sober now for three years and was making amends with a person I had hurt. This person would remain a friend over the course of twenty-three years.

My life continued to evolve when I moved to a one bedroom apartment in Thousand Oaks. Though I obtained a great corporate job, offering amazing health benefits, my weight had gone up to over 360 pounds since getting clean and sober in 2003. In 2008, I had weight loss surgery and dropped a total of 215 pounds- sixteen sizes. Not just physically, but emotionally I was transformed, and others saw it.

Even with this transformation, 2008-2015 brought ups and downs. There was a continued slow healing with immediate family members as I made amends for my behavior while I was using. As I went through the steps over and over, I witnessed my own family accept and acknowledge me as a strong woman and a peacemaker. Having faith and belief in the twelve steps brought me forgiveness from others and allowed me to forgive myself. I occasionally visited Anthony's friend's family who had moved to Riverside County. I learned to accept my role with this family. Throughout the years around birthdays, anniversaries, and holidays I would think of Anthony, but was no longer emotionally needy. The untold truth was, I never forgot what Anthony meant to me or who he was to me. The pain of losing Anthony was indescribable, so I buried it. And it was through this process that I felt a connection with God and began to experience something like grief. Subsequently, my relationship with his extended family improved as I was more present and willing to be a true friend without the expectation of a relationship with Anthony. One night, as I was preparing to go visit my friends in Riverside County, I prayed for help. As I was still, I thought of the words, "Trust me."

As time went on and I grew older, I continued to stay clean and sober. I participated in my life, embracing it as much as I would allow myself to. I wrote letters, hoping to let go, even though It- the ugly, icky stuff was there in me. I was still in contact with Frank, my ex, and although in 2012 we talked about marriage, it was just talk. The reality was, we both knew it was not possible. In my heart I had done my best in our relationship. Marriage would be for the wrong reasons. For the most part, we were not romantically involved and were just friends. Our relationship was often confusing even to the people who witnessed it. We went through long periods of absence though he only lived five miles from me. The result was that we took time outs and regrouped. We made peace and did the best we could. Although there was no romance, we became close without the added drama. We forgave each other and built a friendship of respect and understanding that I still cherish today.

In 2015, I returned to college and was later contacted by an old friend from high school through Facebook named Jeremy. Although we were merely acquainted with each other in high school, we began to get to know each other as adults. We agreed after three weeks of communicating on messenger to meet. We both shared the disappointments of our hearts and told each other about our lives. I shared the story of how I got clean and how I was still hurting. We took our time, did not rush, and waited until our tenth date to kiss.

I fell in love for the first time during my recovery- while for the first time being the best version of myself. I started to experience the things I desired for my life; I made arrangements to introduce him to the family that meant so much to me. The night before visiting them, I prayed to God for peace and as I became quiet, I had a thought again of, "Trust me." The day with the family was filled with laughs and good conversation. I felt a sense of harmony. We took pictures and walked in the park across the street.

One evening after we went to dinner, we were talking about God, and I shared what being Catholic meant to me. Although Jeremy had been married twice, it was important to him to understand what he desired for his own life. I had already been married and divorced for nearly twenty five years, but I knew life was preparing me to be married. Somehow, It- the ugly, icky stuff would still cause me to question myself. I continued to carry burden, blame and shame for the relationships that had come and gone in my life. After attending a self-discovery process together, Jeremy made the decision to go through the same process I went through in 2003. I agreed to sponsor him in the Catholic faith. The process at times was spiritually emotional for both of us. I got to witness the transformation of someone I cared for change for the better. Our love flowered into something magical with God at the center. Yet in 2016, I was told that I'd have to have surgery and that kids would no longer be possible. For whatever reason, I remembered Anthony in that moment of disappointment. The blow of the news automatically made me reference the pain I still carried inside. Yet on Christmas 2016, Jeremy proposed to me, and It- the ugly, icky stuff, was replaced with overwhelming happiness. In April 2017, Jeremy was confirmed in the Catholic faith. The foundation we built our relationship on helped prepare our life together. As we met with various people within the church to go over details of the sacrament, the church required us to attend Engagement Encounter, a retreat for couples getting married.

The process opened my eyes to the commitment I was being called to. I was stressed and exhausted with sadness and mixed emotions as I prepared to move out of my apartment of ten years. The process of letting go was clear to me as I went through my belongings.

That feeling of letting go continued. During the move, we went to a nearby mall to window shop for my birthday. At one point, Jeremy, the kids, and I stopped at a candy store where I noticed a man and a young teenage girl near the chocolate area. When the man turned around, I realized that it was my ex-husband Alex, who I had not seen in years. The kids and my fiancée were introduced. In a few moments it was only Alex and I looking at each other. We embraced and as I looked into his eyes, I sincerely apologized for hurting him. He replied by saying I did not have anything to be sorry for. The forgiveness I felt seemed to have been God given, an overwhelming sense of gratitude.

The days leading up to May 2018 went by fast. Jeremy and I decided that we would have a small wedding, since we both had been previously married. The month of the wedding, I started to feel nervous, like I was running out of time. There was unfinished business still in my heart. It- the ugly, icky stuff awaited. One night I began to cry so much over the doubts that filled my mind that I began to believe that I would always carry this pain no matter how much work I had done. It was what it was. Meanwhile, we moved in together and I took on the role of cooking, cleaning, washing, and shopping for a family of four, which was overwhelming. I knew there was going to be a transition period, but in spite of that, I chose to do everything in our home. It- the ugly, icky stuff was starting to show its face, causing me to feel resentful over all of my new responsibilities. I was exhausted by the end of the day, working and then coming home to work another three to four hours. Instead of continuing to spin, I researched and talked to mothers who had similar experiences and came up with a solution for the family I was about to be married into. I made a list of chores for everyone to commit to which actually worked.

The week of the wedding, my mother flew in, as I asked her to give me away. Having my mother be a part of this day filled my heart with joy. My parents' forty-five year marriage was something I now looked at with great admiration. As a woman, it felt wonderful to be thankful for what each parent contributed to who I was becoming. As I was about to be married, I realized the overall experience of my existence. I had been raised by a mother and father who gave their children love. In the cherished memories of growing up, there was always laughter in the house. On the day of the wedding, I honored my mother for the example she has always been, and remembered my father for his love. I got married, and Jeremy my husband gave me a magical honeymoon.

Strangely, It- the ugly, icky stuff still showed up two months after we returned home from our honeymoon in Hawaii. It appeared by way of social media. Without thinking, I made reference to Jeremy's past relationship, which generated a character assault on me from one of Anthony's friends. Even more painful, they also brought up a comment about him. Although I deleted the post, in that moment, It- the ugly, icky stuff caused me to respond and react poorly. The pain I felt from this was like a knife going in my back. I knew they understood me, as I had not let go. And for that reason, the hurt I felt caused me to weep like I had this coming for a long time. Though we had been married a short time, Jeremy held me as I cried and comforted me, reassuring me that everything was going to be okay. As the months went by, It- the ugly, icky stuff plagued me with thoughts of life and death. I asked God why this situation with Anthony's friend's family had taken place. I began to withdraw from normal daily activities and stopped listening to music. Jeremy then watched helplessly as I went through the deepest depression of my life.

In the fall, I reached out to my sponsor in my twelve step program. They suggested the tenth step- writing about these relationships that consumed me. This step was difficult to write because I had to admit that I was wrong in what had taken place. I did not realize that since getting clean and sober, I actually was giving other people control over my feelings. Yet, I sensed a peace after completing this process.

As Christmas and New Year started of 2019, I still could see that It-the ugly, icky stuff was now coming out in the way I reacted towards my family. I knew I needed to get back to the basics of recovery and start attending mass. Due to a traumatic hand injury that happened at home, I took time off work in June 2019 The injury was in my dominant hand which I began treating through occupational therapy.

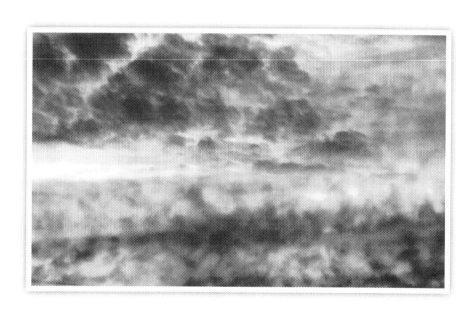

Then, on July 2, 2019, I attended a recovery group and was given a pamphlet on "How to Listen to God" (How to Listen to God by John E Batterson, Oxford group Pamphlet 1930's). It opened my understanding to how big God really is. I thought I already knew this, but this gave me a perspective so much larger than I had. It conveyed something as simple and profound as how to listen. I carried this document with me and read it five times the same day I received it. The next day I had an appointment for car maintenance about 30 minutes away. Though I asked Jeremy to go with me to drop off my car three times, three times he declined, due to being tired. I gathered my belongings and got into my car and made my journey to the car dealership during the golden hour. I was not listening to music, absorbing the quiet and clearing my mind. As I drove and passed the local farms, I heard the inner voice say, "Aren't you tired of it?" I knew what it was referring to.

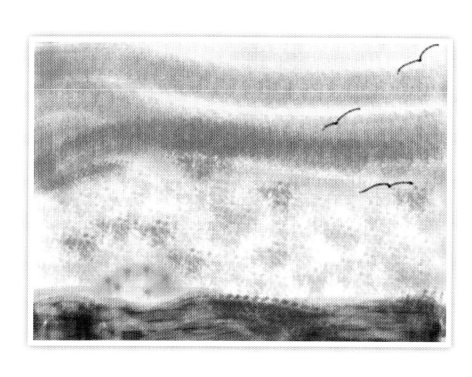

In this moment, I knew the action I needed to take in order to deal with the deep hurt buried within me. I got to the dealership, dropped off my car, and came home. When I arrived, I spoke to a friend who recommended I write about the experience and then shared this with Jeremy. Then I placed myself in a timeout. I grabbed a yellow notebook and pen, then sat on the sofa. I wrote at the top of page: Let go. Let God. In the meantime, certain numbers came to mind, so I wrote them down on the side of the paper. I waited and I waited for a response. The response I received in this exercise was names of people I resented or misunderstood. When I was done writing the names, it became clear what I had been doing to myself and the part I had in my own unhappiness. I knew that I was not trusting God with all my heart. I was not loving my neighbor as I loved myself. I felt a sadness and repented to God for my part in the pain. I decided that I would pray for what I wanted for my own life and for the people on my list. While I was completing errands the next day, I stood in line for Starbucks. A few moments before ordering, a notification popped up on my phone to do an update. Anger and resentment began to rise in me until I heard a little voice, "Watch it, Elizabeth. Resentment is coming back." I told the cashier I was fine paying cash. I smiled and went on with my day. This day and that particular situation was different. When I drove home, it felt like my eyes were finally opened. Everything I was now experiencing- from the aggravations from people, to the smells of flowers, to the sound of birds was captivating and I was overcome with humility and grace. I was in awe of what was given to me, although I still did not understand it all.

The next remarkable situation happened three weeks later while attending a birthday party for a mutual friend. I shared my enlightenment and how my perspective seemed to have changed with another guest. . She mentioned that my overall perspective was called a paradigm shift. But as the afternoon went on, as many people were at the party, I was taken aback from another guest whom I barely knew, but who really did not like me. Three separate times in our interactions I felt uncomfortable. My response was simply to do nothing and act like nothing was going on. I felt an overwhelming sense of understanding and compassion towards this woman. The party was for a mutual friend and it was not the place to bring negativity up. I chose to accept the feelings without placing any judgment. The peace and grace that consumed me felt wonderful as I understood that I was indeed changing. I met new friends and exchanged phone numbers. I connected with another guest named Bella who I confided in about what I was experiencing. She shared a term with me for looking at a situation or person without judgment: Wu Wei. In a later text message from her, Bella explained that it is the ability to be harmonious with others. "According to Daoism, human happiness occurs when one aligns with the Dao, and Wu-Wei allows practitioners of Daoism to live in harmony with one's natural surroundings and to be mindful of the interconnectedness of all life" (www.newworldencyclopedia.org). I managed to learn how to react towards people without compromising myself. I was excited that I experienced Wu Wei three different times in one day. I realized that I had embraced this change to my disposition even though I had no idea about the concept. During this time, I had been feeling an overload of memories, which I dealt with through walks, prayers, watching sunsets, reading the Bible, meditation, and learning Tai Chi.

In addition, being Catholic, I wanted to make sure this did not go against the teachings of the church. The next day, I went for a drive and stopped at a Catholic parish to see if it was possible to see a priest, because I did not have a scheduled appointment. I needed the opinion of a priest about what had been happening. When I arrived at the church, the priest came out and led me to a conference room where we could talk. After a brief introduction, he heard my confession. I began to tell him about the last few weeks. I mentioned the pamphlet I was given and the title of it. He said, "Before you arrived I was reading an article sent by a website I subscribed to for priests." The title of what he was reading was "How to Listen to God." He nodded his head in agreement, validating the experience I was having. To him, this was a confirmation that I was speaking the truth. Our faces mirrored smiles, as we both knew how powerful God is.

In conclusion, the life lessons I was learning were not wasted, even while I was going through the pain. The good choices I made, from getting involved in a twelve step program to a belief which turned into hope, faith, and love for God have all led me to who I am today. I have learned that focusing more on my relationship with God gives me a better understanding of myself and others around me. As I became more willing to be healthy and balanced in my relationships with others, I gained a new freedom. We all have one life to lead. No matter what our differences: religion, age, sexual orientation, body type, race, or gender. We are all here to have a spiritual experience. The journey is at everyone's own pace, because we learn differently. The world consists of seven billion unique people, presenting opportunities to learn from one another's differences. But what we all share is the same desire- to be loved and to give love.

*Elizabeth Grant*

*The End*

# BIBLIOGRAPHY

1. English Standard Bible, Prov. 3.5) "Trust in the Lord with all your heart"

2. John E Batterson, Oxford group Pamphlet 1930's) "How to Listen to God"

3. (www.newworldencyclopedia.org) "Daoism, Wu-Wei

4. (Rite of Christian Initiation of Adults) RCIA

5. A twelve-step program is a set of guiding principles outlining a course of action for recovery from addiction, compulsion, or other behavioral problems. www.winkipedia.org

6. Tai chi (Chinese: 太極; pinyin: Tàijí), short for T'ai chi ch'üan or Tàijí quán (太極拳), is an internal Chinese martial art practiced for both its defense training, its health benefits and meditation. www.winkipedia.org

For more interviews, speaking and questions on the writings in this book. Please email egrant52018@gmail.com

Printed in the United States
By Bookmasters